Success of the Seed Plants

To Andrew —

with best wishes!

Leslie

10 November 2010

SUCCESS OF THE SEED PLANTS

Leslie williams.

Leslie Williams

Bellday Books, Inc.

Durham, North Carolina and Pittsburgh, Pennsylvania

Published by Bellday Books, Inc., P.O. Box 3687, Pittsburgh, PA 15230; www.belldaybooks.com

Cover and interior design by Cassandra Patten.

Library of Congress Cataloguing-in-Publication Data

Williams, Leslie.
        Success of the Seed Plants: poems / Leslie Williams.
            p. cm.

        ISBN 978-0-9793376-3-5

1. Americans-Poetry. I. Title.
Library of Congress Control Number 2010911692

TO
my person

FOR
my boys

CONTENTS

❖

❖❖

❖❖❖

FOX IN THE LANDSCAPE

Tulip, you
Bled on my green rug.

A jungle-red petal
Where my little kits

Rollick, fallen like a warning—

Yesterday I sat outside
In the returned sun

Trying to make more
Friends; after all these years

To think of yourself
Snapped, the sweet sap

Tremoring between
States of ice and melt.

An old love wrote to me
From his wife's country place

To say he had been hunting there
And could appreciate the hounds;

In a white coat he is closely
Setting people's bones, opening

Their backs with the hands
I knew

The cancelled paths
Of saying no or yes: I could have fallen

To a fearing of the little foxes lately
Come into the yard

(There is so little I know about what to do)
But I let them be.

SMALL DIASPORA

From exuberant hanging gardens
populous with knaves—

rakes, lotharios, libertines,
paladins, princelings, brigands, rogues,
paramours, suitors, swain—

right now everywhere
corn-fed boys are lacing cleats
and spilling out of dugouts,

(bound in the willow
a certain strain)

right now in sacred jars
a clutch of early text,

— beaux, coxcombs, gentlemen, flame—

right now driving down a street never
seen before,

my little sons buckled into booster seats
wearing superhero capes.

I like their attitude!

I like the salty parks crew
that brings more soil
for the neighborhood, away

across the river from
the disapproving dames—

where dilettantes can simply
take delight,

and amateurs make their way
with only the authority of love.

OPEN AS

a seed cracking in land,
root-hairs slipped through to surfeit
on a netherworldly soup.

Of this euphoria, much before: bluegrass
festivals over in Syria, Virginia
breakfasts on the tinware— a claiming
sunlight striking the plates— overly
vivid, the scrambled eggs, the coffee pot,
stray memory-scraps still speak— by
the creekbed, in the three-day camp
where they came to build fires.

Tell me: are you comfortable?

Never knowing when you're going
you'll be going back: a single day
in mind a thousand thousand times.

Knowing what will happen, not exactly *how*.

If you're still reading give me a sign
and I will find you: ruined, shoeless at the door
of the yellow apartment. One night of rueful, would
that do it? Are you still beautiful?

THE RAKE

Spring is sprung
from winter's prison!
Jaybirds announce my wantonness:

Sweeping in with a gray
rain coat, whistling
like brass through plucky

glades, I let vapors
out to graze and ogle
all that grows.

Iris commands
the onion-weed scatter
under her blue flags;

tulips nudge
into hooded pleasure
as tiny crocus crop up

frivolous at dogwoods' feet—
I see they have red
lips for the bees. And there,

in meretricious yellow,
forsythia waves
wands of unbidden, unbridled

hair— unaware
of what she asks, going out
dressed like that.

The Brambles, the Glossy Black Fruit

We drive over the mountain to see
Johnny and his land, thick
with blackberries. I wear a hat, and borrow
Johnny's jeans to avoid getting scratched.

The man I am with
fights the briary patch, trying
to put the best in my bucket,

but Johnny just plucks them off, sweet,
and hands them to me.

Each plump explosive lolls
on my tongue before it bursts, letting go grainy wine—
each berry alone is its own
bunch of elfin grapes.

As we climb into the truck to leave, I
feel as I have ever felt, but pricked
with a tiny infidelity
carried in the tub of glistening fruit.

On the drive home I don't look away
from the bright ball of sun, even though I know
I'm supposed to.

LETTER FROM FARMVILLE

Moon-dipped night on irregular cool
flagstones: in a hand-me-down night-
gown and stretching the sleeves.

In neighboring barns the locals work
like oceans at night. Heavy and with salty
tongues. Stoic kids with histories, marked

for sacrifice. Black sheep. They say little,
a riptide coursing underneath, to which I
gravitate. One more rapture aimed for

dissolved by daybreak, the horses impatient
for a groom to appear. Surely something weightier
will come to pass in other hemispheres:

in a steamy glass room on top of a mountain
for example, decibel and revelry— while outside
breath-stealing air stings through, bracing and frozen.

I intend to stop being in touch.

DISSECTION

I.

Lifting sheets of *dura mater,* the novice
gasps, a momentary captive of this rapt
geography: a sheep brain's pucker and crease,
braille terrain of a half-pound moon,
gray oddment from the slaughterhouse.

Slicing mottled slickness, her scalpel jounces
over ruts, jaunty as a horse-drawn cart,
cleaving gum of *corpus callosum* so halves
fall away, baring the shrubbed interior.

II.

Fragile thought: a farm woman drives
a cart, sets hens and sows the lettuces.
She goes to collect the eggs, and the ewe
in the field witnesses her departure.

Now years later, in the lab, the student
flinches as a squirt of cerebral fluid hits
her face. In this juice the useless, nameless
memory was stored, an observation
whose chemicals still cling, a sensory
impulse of the ewe, who patiently blinked
and chewed, not waiting for this trifling truth to out.

III.

At the sink the student rinses formaldehyde
away, dumps from her tray the unraveled
halves, remains; it is evening.

Walking home alone across unleafy
quads, a dim rumination sputters at her mind,
trapped in a gibbous divide without fire
to forge such harrowing alliances—
glistening, so stainless.

NIGHT SWIMMING

The tartness of winesaps augurs true fall:
a smack and tang of attenuated air
at the top of Brown's Mountain, sprawled
across the whole ache of sky, where

the small pond's a salver of stars
and for an exquisite instant, I'm an infant
feeling all: each star's sliver at the heart,
each minnow an arrow in ink— and

how a pond can save stories, stay
starflooded, lightbearing, old,
as we drop through layers of lake
to the bottom: a cold eye.

On Finding One's Neighbor Dead in His Garden

No one saw the clumsy way his body
hit the ground: a crumpled slump, splay
of spade and elbows, face down— now starkly
motionless against the riffling play
of wind lifting lank strands of hair. Near
the bed stand grand hydrangeas, forgotten
in their pots, each swaying nod a boutonniere
whose blue brooding stuns the narrow plot,
heavy with bees and shadowed by a hollow throat
of steeple, white with sun. He must've swooned
when the hive stirred, gathering its fierce coats
in a dancing, dazzled shroud. How soon
warm earth prints him like a wrinkled sheet—
brown, soft, tired, kissing— cheek to cheek they meet.

She understood something of the dying oaks,
their gothic traceries rootbound and grave.

But how did branches tap the sky
with such arthritic spires, and will the spirit out?

Since her mother's throat unstopped a cry
like a foal in the night, she'd been first

of her kind in these hills. Sometimes a dark
horse surprises and wins: a summer hill

unfolds again in gold dusklight and she flies
from the back of Earth, left for dark

in Virginia's spelled heart, hoof-sweet—
while boundless July, laden with evenings, returns

with trinkets and wares, trundles out to her farthest
field with all the stars finespun, coming on—

the still pool still fringed
with goldenseal, with scuppernong.

ACRE

Trespass   balefire
Darkness of a building storm

Company for the falling in
Homestead   spinster sisters

On the porch in wraith dress
To receive

Mud rutted by wheel
Stamped horseshoes

A parchment erased for the purpose
Of using the parchment again

Remnant games of gin
A dusty jar

Run through in twilight
Dominion   of acts already

Waxen as magnolia   fires
Blazing around the property

When the new tenants
Drive up   an immense

Privacy interrupted
Upturned canoe

(Tell me everything)

LETTER FROM MONTICELLO, 1801

By now you must be almost to Washington,
fleeting over hilly land— and I
am a pebble of ice, hail
on your horsehoof,
a stone under saddle— *Sally, Sally,*
night after night, *goodbye.*
I am wax, I am tallow
and bloodless in a mulberry bed.

Remember one of those last
cold nights, how we spirited
a glowworm over frozen garden
where your peas will twine
snapped sweetness
in spring? I said *I want no more*

to remember, a crushed
coal in my body hardening
its many-edged regret.

Tonight I lie too long
on my back outside

sweeping dark arms through snow.

POND, THE VULNERABLE

extremity, frozen,
thawing, wonder-
ful; the moon has fallen
in. It keeps all doomed
commitments, crucial
and particular, hinged
on single rupturings
of fate's ascendant bloom.
Tonight, the ravaged
elms, a fresh calf wobbly
(pond ice, new knees)
and whining to her mother
who calmly eats
the placenta, steaming.
Even they know how
it ends. And old women,
crimped way they spend
a life, gnarled hands
making do. Like nocturnal
eyes they are paying
attention to blackness
and begin to home in, begin
to be perfectly alone
with the face of the calf
fallen through, open
eyes bloodflecked
like feldspar, moonstones
full of bald world.

In Me as the Swans

Not embittered
even while freezing
to the ice of their own lakes.

The night I was leaving for Madrid
into the noisy party a dazzling
friend-of-a-friend walked in: I want so much
(as a couple of kids on the dance floor want)
to slow the tempo, hold there longer,
to feel that seedly longing
to be pressed into the soil,
or that little lift the mothers get
when stocking larders, even now,
vestige of the primitive urge
to be provided for and to provide.

      I went alone to see that balcony
in Verona, after the Roman dramas and luxuries
above the Spanish Steps, when an elegant
footman brought a pack of Reds on a silver
tray and all but smoked them for you,
after your towels had warmed in London's best
hotel, whose name I can't remember and am kind of glad,
glad now for the rest of empty August and
the convent hostel's eleven o'clock curfew,
glad now when I go to the distinguished dinners
that I have stood alone
wondering at illuminated books,
looking at Woolf's spectacles under glass
or standing under Bourgeois's giant spider
at the Tate— at times the best kept universe
was my own, no interceding docents
or guided tours, but a riverine serendipitous
wandering— waif, naïf.

      I liked the light enormously so why
did I obey the bell that called me in?

When I last see S. he's bursting in late for rehearsal,
throwing back massive cathedral doors
with a *clank*, loud as klieg lights hamping on,
throwing light into the hushed nave
where the small figures already gathered
turn in slow surprise. Or was the last time
in a doorframe(?): fresh from the shower,
white shirt damping slightly on his chest,
cuffs and neck open, his elegant hands.

I want all of this to count, not just be vestige—
to have attached, and for good reason. Not kept simply
because it streamed through my body's two cubic feet,
but for purposes of record— vivid, comprehensive
and made from each grazing and accretion: those rocks, this
person, that state line, these sheets. When my body
enters in the yard de-atomizing, resolving, burning a pit
shaped like itself, let it be fueled by the thrill-
flooded annals within, the blood in every leaf.

HANDSOME FLOWERS IN MOUNTAINOUS REGIONS

I wanted to talk more—

But I took a shower and left my friend
Because that's what we had planned

(Lonely so close to lovely)

Down road poured through rock, wind falling in
The turns, and never going back

Not even to visit lonesome Aunt Florene

In her stone house with a view of the gap
And the old-time candies in cellophane—

Huge cold rhododendrons true dwellers there.

A stranger said in the meeting hall:
Some of these stories too sad to say.

If I could just correct
The mountains I'm a daughter of:

How they shamed me
By shrewd discipline of not wanting things.

What, in the end, shall be required of me?
Which is my purview, bailiwick, district,

Scene? What my bounden territory? Why are these
My flaws, that do not go well with life— and why

Such balm in the round bales of hay, or in a name
Printed plainly in a borrowed book?

I HAD BEEN SO LOVE TO YOU

Marion   thank you for your restaurant
in the dead-eye of North Carolina

And for the biscuits I've taken
from the table and hidden in my purse

Stormclouds boiling in the sky   bringing me
past ills   resplendencies   all this way

Take the kind of conversation
outside on library bricks as the sun would
disappear unnoticed

Or the college kids who came for dinner
and left me with the dishes   I stayed up too late
finding the lost mitten

Many more times will fail
the night blizzard and the candler's wish
to have sung more

Thou who made the storm   prove me
in the detours   purposeful

Remember me the two lakes

PICNIC SUPPER, THE BLUFFS

The Blue Ridge spreads its gingham
in our laps, where green is good
and God— let us thank Him

for the open-meadow gleam, the cabin
we can hardly see (on the valley floor
below), the bobcat tracks, the feel

of sunburned rocks at dusk in Doughton
Park. And for Roosevelt's Civilian Corps,
who toiled here once in the blue-eyed grass.

Tonight we have pimiento cheese
and BLTs, crushed ice. We revel
in the dark, happy as spleens.

The blue blood of fall
can't yet run its course
through us, though the ring

of stones is darkening. Heaped-up
green banks, like loaves
of earth, enclose a natural fort.

Ha! We're caught in the teeth of the moon.

OCTOBER WITH OLD MASTERS

I am not finished
Gorging on the verdure of July—

Dear cathedral architects,
I'm often sure we'll be received
In a big Delft sky,

Though the world's accomplished
Physicists say there's no place

To put an afterlife:
Eleven dimensions already

Accounted for, according to
My dinner partner over soup.

We need more ingenious eyes, you
Servants to the table, gold vinaigrette
With maker's mark, objects of vertu—

Tell about the soldiers
And the mothers, whose infants

Died and still the milk
Soaked whole gowns through—

I cried at the Mauritshuis
And in the Gemäldegalerie:

Sir, the thunderstorm's my
Province, for I have careless
Loved it.

PARABLE

I miss the kind of friend whose vices
won't retreat in middle age;

I miss weather in a supporting role,
mayflies and the cold pool.

And the madness of the hill towns,
creamed chicken and cornbread

and underneath these, pain's strange, wiry variety—
I could be something more, more serious.

At times I even miss the city's never-ending
hours, autocratic, always possible to be

turned out of an apartment by the heat
and so to wander aimlessly, the avenues at night.

Even birds can find the sanctuary set aside for them.

Work of the smallest lives can change
sugar into alcohol or leaven bread.

A mustard grain can grow into the greatest
shrub, to give the wicked shade.

FROM THE TOP

In the car on the way to the naked hot springs
brown bottles chink in a paper bag.

Soon we will submerge in steaming stone pools
our blithe bodies below
the delicious flare of cold.

Frosty morning, storm drain.

We will lie on the white bedspread in the rented
room, we will be damp and loose-limbed;
we will not hurry.

I will overhear a woman—

I am carrying her story for all these days
like the rusty buckle on my shoe.

— A man asking, and her answers: no,
the neighbors raised a barn. My son's fourteen.

I will think it's OK to fold into myself
for a while, to need cake
doughnuts and milk in the coffee, be
devoted to unreadiness.

You show me the houses that went belly-up
high on the mountain, almost
above the tree line.

For all these days I am carrying
a view: bare frame structures, flapping
Tyvek, stacks of lumber. An immaculate
gasping air.

IN WHICH SHE IS UNMOVING

Tucked in, a woman hears the night
trucks trafficking the Interstate, hauling
free-range chickens and aspirin. On the dark

there is reliance. And on the mental lengths
of rope that tether disparate events
and make them next-of-kin.

Who can consider a river and not think
of letting things run their course, the rocks
in the bed and how much between them.

Once in a crowded lecture hall
the celebrated teacher pronounced the sting
of love "the pain of being two."

Later that year she saw him walking in the rain
looking wildly diminished, a feeble old man
in a mouse-colored coat. Astonishing,

that friends she'd bathed, or cried with,
still breathe in this world— just now sleeping
or eating an omelette or touring ancient towns.

EPHESUS

Hasam in his peach-colored shirt
waited with us on the dusty side of the road
for the bus. When it silvered on the horizon
he hoisted our bags, then tossed them
through a cloud of exhaust and dust
into the cargo door, unhurried. A vaccination
scar flashed its perfect circle on his forearm
and we embraced, my dress blooming
in the breeze.
                    I wish I had asked
that young Turk who drove us from Ephesus
to Priene and Miletus on the tour groups' off day,
who waited below blasting pop radio in his Italian car
as we pantomimed myth in Diana's high resiny temples,
alone in cicadas' drone and circle— I wish I had asked
how he survives the silted-up harbors, sod-sunken
marble, endless orange Fantas and idleness.

How does he abide the vivid tomatoes
in boarded trucks rolling through Ionian dust,
women working the fields fully veiled,
unwrapping their lunches in the shade?

DREAMS IN CROWDS *(Tomorrow I May Be Far Away)*

Years of serendipity— proximity for mixing
And sneaking through the saw grass, bittersweet—

So long I've been saying to the house, lying down
On all the beds and looking out each window.

Dust is made from everything, even cosmic stuff and bits of iron.

I might have thrived less constantly on summer
Heat, a closeness with the midnight radio, the birds that only remind.

I'm still holding for the hour, storied room within the rooms,
For my core till now intractable to form

Into a better pattern. I want to be mistaken

Re: an instant changing all— phone call
Or a dashing visitor, deciding to stay on.

I want to stop believing that and waiting for it too.

ELSEWHERE, I SAY

merciful, that what went on there still goes on
in me: repooling the moon into bathtub,
repeated descending of stairs. I got close

enough to answer the door, start coffee,
set out the knives and carving board. As far
as the galley, whose bottles wore little nametag

necklaces on silver chains: (Hello, I'm Gin).
But I do not know enough to limn that life, pick up
where I left off, brief realms of unquenchable

charm. How easily I knew your body: kittenly,
love-ish; if I had gotten any nearer I would
know it still, as traveled as the route

from Stony Point to Troutman, a furnished
life unsearched for, like the quartz
as big as doorstops that turned up in your fields.

September, Already

And they say I am no better.

After picking tomatoes
the ripe stink blooms
in my hands.

While people are up at the house
I ease my limbs into fall water.

Shrill echoes widen
across the night lake.
My head is small,
an oval bathed in fog,

the moon's fruit slipped
from its skin.

No, Then Yes

In warmer times
all life was aqueous

in shallow seas that flooded
continents and then

an archipelago arose
whose rocks today

lie scattered
from Wales across

to Newfoundland and
down along the Eastern

Seaboard of U.S.
where beaches

and the sea floor
gained eroded fine

remains of mountains
that in another era

lived alone in air

DARESAY

Every morning I try it—
On the beach with borrowed kite

On the beach in nightclothes, empty cup
Cool sound, sand's susceptible forms—

Columns of rain pour into horizon, not here.

In Manteo there must've been an original
Sense of awe, a scenery

Arresting, so majestic— what they saw,
Arriving in hulks of wooden boats

With porridge, disease, daily pain—
No time to pick their heads up, for very survival.

My grandmothers would have every right
To judge me harshly, content as I am to idle

While they were ruined for leisure, constantly
Spreading tablecloths and winding clocks—

Every morning I try the dream
Of biking away from Johnnie Mercer's pier

Unmediated, the arcade just a place to read
The morning paper, the pomegranate a weightless fruit.

I'm ruined another way, ruined away

Last night we talked about the idea we got
Growing up: people either had Success

Or didn't, not much changing it. A rowboat

Dredged in sand without *whose* or *whether* or *when.*

You know what I'm sayin'?

Even the woman at Robert's grocery store
Spoke to me like a friend.

BE HONEST

The phone rang after eleven p.m.; past clearing dishes
I was naked under a throw, crocheting, obsessed with who was
trying to reach me from a noisy bar. The call was from L.A., *hello?*
Wanted to say a name. But no, he's dead,
dead yesterday, in a bathroom three time zones

away. Glassine envelope, head to lip of pedestal sink. His face
in the obit is so various: aloof and wounded, deep-running-
water-still. Oh so easy on the eyes. Oh— the way he wore
a shirt, the only one of them who could be counted on.
The kind of man (calling him *man* a quiver, a sting)

to solve me. How to say burning? I was timbers, a house
on stilts. On Woods Hole's obfuscated wharf, a desperateness;
be honest. He said the *Rosa rugosa* near the ferry had fighting
leaves, a sudden toughness in its hips. I'll make his favorite
lunch (tomato soup, a sandwich) and leave it by the dock

because I could never be
an actor, waiting for my cue, while gorgeous stormcloud
morning shades do layer in like oil. This kind of hot,
a thunderstorm incipient. A solar wind.

So Long

From every widow's walk the view is weathervane,
risen up from cupolas to punctuate
Nantucket's hooked shape. Here in the glossy

upper reaches (hammock, lilac and hydrangea), sea
weather beats on shingles and lamplit singing lessons,
rains out bad tennis. But how to save it from

nostalgia? Resist, *resist* the blueberry pail, kitchen
stools pulled knee to knee, blue teeth, blue grins, all
ignorance. So long, you jubilant revelers at Thirty

Acres, the bicycle I rode to the airport, that first
taste of Cape Cod. In the Whaling Museum—
amid a two-story jawbone, scrimshaw and harpoons—

lies a wife's terse letter: "Where is the axe?"
beside her husband's reply, two years too late:
"Look in the shed." How severe even love

was then: no halter tops, no spicy Bloodys
sprigged with celery. No drinks called hurricanes,
no falling in love as aftermath, no glorious
hungover dawn, wobbling home on a bike.

THE FAMOUS DIRECTOR SAID *I LOVE TO SEE PEOPLE COMING
OUT OF DARKNESS*

The woman at the party who had been married to him
had the strangest eyes, her irides ringed
with black, then white, then black again, like the eyes of a bull.

I was only half well then,
a monoxide star drawing every time
I'd linger in the garage—

I who so loved comfort
was kept alive thereby,
unable to make a choice or withstand the smallest pain.

She said to me, a stranger:
It's strange what we will do
to get what we want,

or what we do when we don't know
what we want, which is most of the time
unless we're cold or very hungry.

She said she met him outside her apartment
where he parked his bike; he was going home
to put back together what he'd torn apart

the day before in a self-destructive fit, but instead
they went to Jenkins's and drank and danced
in their cowboy boots and smashed bottles against

the wall—she took it for granted while it was going on,
a form of imperative, the top-of-the-mountain stuff
she never doubted at all.

She left me with the opinion of herself
that she had been completely open,
though, she came to believe, not from a Healthy Place.

She left me willing to be crushed again
beneath the wheels, each meal a kind of viaticum
to grasp, to seize, be fed by hand,
to be combusted by the sound of a voice
or a savage attitude.

The place a carnassial love creates, where we go
if we're called to, that kind
of courage— to go again
to his body, his cross tattoo—

after her funeral I knew I was afraid
but nowhere can I prove
that I slipped away from the visitation and went to him
in the almost empty house, how I felt standing at the door
inside my stockings and modest dress before he answered it.

for *Naked Ladies*. And the hothouse is smutty
with blooms. These lascivious amaryllises

are falling out of their painted pots, overwrought
among the heady stench of mulch. The opposite

of topiaries— girlish ivies pruned and trained
to hug wire frames— these light-headed bulbs

husbanded their own pubescence in the dark.
Underground. Now their free flowering goes on

forever: green swords thrust forth from a seed
of shyness; they become and become. Embarrass

like erotica, show off. They show, in blowsy sprays
of sheen that clothe the shaft then drop. No

amaranth, this flower has a willingness
to waste. We all know places we'll never fit in.

But a flower like this? All power, no fear.
This flower is out for itself. Full velveteen throttle.

This flower is not my fault.

Two Hydrogens, One Oxygen

Rain, hear
it stinging the frost-top, sizzling the ice
crust; a sound like singing, singeing; mini-insects
leaping: snowhoppers under lobes
of cedar bowing with white loads.

Wet is dripping through the honeycombs
of window screen (the zinged
metallic smell) and in the droplet

trapped there floats a copy of the woods beyond
the soft horse track,
these woods that belonged
to you, lovers who
roamed here— grass-stained,
pine-pitched— glad
bodies for to sing & sing. Not one of you
conclusion.

O, minutiae
that are part of mental annals!

Such as: I still know what your father
said, driving you to boarding school.
Grudging scrap of history I've taken up
as a plant sucks water
and makes a leaf of it. Substantiated.
That is, my braincase carries you.
It is my favorite idea.

Like Zelda

How long has it been since she woke up
high in back of a turnip truck, the downtown
streets scrimmed with dawn? Among cool

tumbling mounds just pulled from decorous
drowsing underground— as she was
pulled in: impossible spin, unthinkable

only hours before, dressing simply
for the night. Such alchemies of reveling
(the devastating loveliness) made

for time's vital split: all she wanted, right
then. Amazed, wavering in powder rooms'
gilt glass: *Who am I to have a part in this?*

— Blandishments, whole cities snatched, mirrored
platters of nacreous shells— inside, each glittering
demise. Taken whole, like lovers before

words. Elixirs of fast sweet slurp and easy
slide, raw but clean of grit. In love then,
behaving in ways fueled only by love, euphoric—

too electrified to eat. Unhealthy as raw
nerve. Now whatever happens next
can never be as marvelous.

LIGHT A CANDLE, PUT IT UNDER A BOWL

Dear Catherine with your arms filled up with lilies—
such intoxicant perfume!— this prophetic
question I need answered today:

how can austerity be the way
when most of what we know is gained
by saying yes, dear Anchoress—

does not exhilaration consecrate, a pure
exuberance the same as selflessness we're striving for
each day (that kind of joyful which the bitter

do so actively disdain)— and when will it
arrive, that promised leaping in the chest,
freemartin with lustrous eyes— to prove

we cannot seize what must be given freely,
and that the good must be at least as beautiful
as the beautiful? This is why I got confused.

Anodos looked through the door to timeless and brought no message back.

Adonis with his drops of blood made the white rose
Red, his goddess in her swan-drawn car so splendidly
Alone— a brightness come from ashes—

Now our latter-day Narcissus is on the brownstone steps
Lately returned from a journey, nothing to do,

His rejected courtesan on an airplane home,
Nursing a drink so splendidly alone— ashes down
From brightness— she had watched her love,

An actor, making love on screen, seen his avid
Body, undulating muscles, eyes fate-fired as Russian
Novels, full of risk. Eyes so full she had to turn

Away. She in any case had never been his "lover."
He would only be surrendered to some
Lips like morphine-honey, a drip that never, never

Stopped, though he swore the ceaseless flow
Of luxury, services, goods, young women hysterically
Groomed, did not impassion him— she could

Follow him but could not speak. She would
Be planting purple hyacinths. She had been
Open as a camera, so a lot got in.

From the Index of Dark Glamour

Cicadas
  bloodless, passionless, how like the gods
  kept in cages like little birds
  males, metallic voices of

Grey-eyed dream
  white white bed

Shetland
  islands
  pony for the child
  sweater she wore in the sad photo

Slippers
  glass

Suppers
  little, what became of them

Tangerine
  color of her silks

YOUR CITY FALLS DOWN SO BEAUTIFULLY

Earth's whole dispassionate atmosphere
the only thing we now share—

you rushed for the train from Baltimore
and then we were kissing on the train

balanced between the cars, starry
night kissing all those hours—

animus to anima, hand and clay
all that would happen, or that ever had

lit in that small division
of time seized by itself, the longed-for

explanation nearly given up for dead,
panther prowling just for me,

the highest mark, the hour I believed—

no doubt now in your reconstituted
life (a friend said yesterday, almost

cheerfully: *It's your life, what's the big deal!*)
you will have grown to like it—

at last knowing what everyone knows
and nothing more.

PRESSING FLOWERS

In what is now a stranger's house
The book with dried petals remains.

Even love would have died
Between the hidebound pages—

Scamper   scapegrace   scapula   scar

It is wrong to introduce the wayward to the lilies,
Tell them they can dream,

Decide, become— while dropping out of summer
School to get more daytime sleep—

In the forest, reading under falling
Trees, it would be the same for us

Scarlet   scatter   scavenger

Small human numbers
Come across unchurched, unschooled,

The wolf child now in studies
Being groomed for news— it was your roses

Carried to the book,
In a time not looking for goodness.

WHEN THE SKY FALLS WE SHALL HAVE LARKS
— Old Proverb

In sunstruck, in calm lea
Lay your head my expert citizen—

How similar our strategies:
To ravish each day as if the last

Or to go about each as if it lasts
In ordinary splendor, on and on, forever—

In both cases suitable to be
    Besotted,
    Histrionic,
    Profligate,
    Direct;

In any field it takes ten years
To develop mastery; so it should be

That virtuosos throng the boulevards. I am
Looking for them. I am looking to go forth

Again among the young, on whom
Everything depends and is wasted.

Innocenti sleep in her body as
embryos float in a jar. Not to be
coaxed into lambs. Never knock-kneed,
nor nicked for wool to be carded into yarn.
No narcotic click of knitting. But she wore
their spurious warmth for years, wrapped
in self-deceit: the still-possible girl,
inchoate, artlessly making clover chains
in a field of acrid wild onions. It's a field
where she wants to lie down. Under
cottonwoods, while soft stuff grows.
Tasting herbs she's procured in the woods.

She'd briefly studied medicine for its tinctures
and odd names: *Bright's Disease. Proud
Flesh.* She believed in the rightness of names
and in a perfect failure. In a litter for
conveyance, a new leaf. In the will-o'-the-wisp
and the clean flame of cremation, too close
in name to be creation's antonym: not
fair for fire to make quick work of them.
She'll find her woolly field again, let her body
seep in slowly, wholly, cell by cell;
return to her own back yard and ordinary
needs: sweet spring beneath a bedroom
window, blowing muslin, the formulaic
pane. To go back and receive it all like a wafer.

ECSTATIC TRACES

The boredom of rolling cigars

                              as relieved by birdsong—

Racehorses at exercise on packed earth

Cold scent of snowdrops gathered in jars

At the garage sale when she proved the stereo still worked

The soft waltz music gave a grace to people lifting

Books or holding her clothes against their bodies

A quarter for a whole new world to slip on

Waiting for the coffee   always to think of the scars

Her young arms again

Thieves taking backpacks from the front of the café

Stopping for a glass of rosé   friend made on the train

What can I tell you   no Eurail Pass no Marseillaise

Blown rose windows   blue fish of Aix

.

Hundreds for hours squandering alfresco

Almost everyone in summer dresses

.

What can I tell you

Her body lying up in the hill

In loneliest east Tennessee

FIRST FRUITS

It must be that when God speaketh
He should communicate not one thing, but all things.
— Emerson, *Self-Reliance*

While waiting to be seated
An intimation came to me

Exacting, clear, brief
And not by ordinary sight

As if again the color green
Was first discerned by primate eyes

Or the original avocado split

The pit surrounded by such
Smooth halves, salted

First taste on a splendid hill
A kind of losing

Once exotic now crucially
Constituent to me

— This odd exuberance
What I had to give—

The trouble of coming to be
In full the way one's made

The fruit complete
Straight from the skin

The pit a lovely piece
of broken firmament.

THE FLOWER OF THE WHEAT

From the wintered eye
of further nor'easters,

a future-day July is floating
already formed across

the not-yet-spavined
bridge, small turf island

on top of which the picnics and
well-laid macadam paths—

(I've been
                    not a very good friend)

The lonely is the only
wife for me, with me lovingly

to stand against the afternoon's
strike, the secret vigilance

of keeping sadness hidden in
its winding sheet— when battling

one's own weakness is not recognized
as strength— though here

the children gave me an idea
(the certainty) that I must try for them

to have both bread and foxgloves.

wheeled by in afternoons
indelible   as in the time   redressed

one rose on a trellis in the morning   drenched and blazing
thrown open   overblown   walking home
one child dropped off at nursery school
infant in the stroller   hours floating
on chronic impoverished sleep   amid which now and then can open
a small crystalline reprieve   a kind of seeing

you   rose I cannot say enough   blown but hanging on
afraid of   undue love   of solitude
rose on the fence in morning dew   not fooling anyone   not trying to

feed a newborn in the hurricane   elms thrashing bending deep
deep nights I could see Ann's light on in *her* baby's room
across backyards pieced as pie   a comfortable remove
from striving   unable to do more than

a neighbor girl in the cooling dark
riding her yard-sale rocking horse on the dollhouse lawn
whooping whinnying   eyes wild glass

her mother gone in after taking care of a dead bird in the yard
matter of fact   scooped into a plastic bag and put into the trash

sight rose   entryway   rooted rose
along the path   a kind of explanation

rose blooming in the wastes
no one did ever see

RING OF FIRE

I set my coffee cup on the *Better Homes*
and Gardens and went out to shovel snow.

On the White House Tour Jackie said
Everyone should have fresh flowers in the home—

Why do we give so often as a reason
Because I grew up that way, the branching

Age lived up-close and curious
So that everything grows particular and cast: as dies

Rolled out on baize, as dyed indigo in wool, as dying are
The women still listening to Johnny Cash with stubborn

Child-bride solitude, plumb-line through
The later pain— would we love squalor if that were all

We knew? What is taken in to make us, both bread
And the involuted potency of roses—

Waiting at the traffic light today it took me by surprise
To see my little son out walking with his class,

Each child holding to the rope.

could be where there is most to fear.
The scene: a floppy garden hat in beige,
her exquisite ropy neck taking the sun.
A star-nosed mole in the cat's soft
mouth, that limp surrender. She could go
so easily, swept off by a cartoon Wind
whose curlicued breath bursts clouds.
How long has it been here, the same dirt
once floor to a sea, laced with mineral
possibility? And how long the knot
inside her ovary, shiny eggplant
swaying on its thready stem?

ECSTATIC DIAGNOSIS

My children's cantaloupe looks sick—
its beige head tinged with green, dented
from immodest lying on one side,
a dirty sphere patterned with pale nets
like the microscopic fibrin in a clot
stopping blood cells on the loose—

Today a broadcast e-mail urged us all
to make a Death Plan, i.e., goals. It's unfair
to ask me to appear by teleconference or
to make the presentation, when I can barely
brush my teeth or be trusted with machinery—

The reason I'm depleted and my raison d'être both
are you, dear fairest little trompe l'oeils, little morsels,
plump eclairs, the absolute, you perfect deviled eggs,
coins dropped, my sweet gumballs, oh loves—

I am smitten, smote by the globe
of glass that hangs here, light tentacular
and alive, radix, by same route from which Eve came,
pomme blonde on a fainting couch
and reckoning with stings, needing

Whaleroot, ambergris, some medicinal poultice
to handle those subjects that can hold forever
in a kind of thrall, when one lacks the bold
destructive urge but is in possession of the mild,
when what I need is an atomic
                              fever chart, a guide.

To the Chinese the Peach Means Long Life

Nothing feels easy as slipping back to old things.

Yet how attractive splitting is: clean of it and free.
How attractive, when things complicate: cut out,
jump into cars, roar off.

How attractive, the peach trees. The peach trees
a subfamily of roses. Also apricots,
cherries and plums.

The ovary becomes the fruit.

The seed, hidden in the pit. Relationship of flesh
to stone is free- or cling-.

Tao, meaning peach, is found
in writings from 5th century B.C.

A rift in the earth tastes of fruit trees
watered too much. A rift in the earth

is slurried wet with dirt and dislodged
molecules shooting up olfactories: the smell
of peaches lifting from the soil.

Tao, as you know, means *way* or *road*.

ECSTATIC ETYMOLOGIES

Tryst   a station to which the game was driven
To meet their ends

Became   two occluded characters
In evening dress   sneaked away

From dreams in crowds with no one else let in   crowds in dreams

In rooms awash with light   vulnerable yet not at all afraid

Herd   stampeded   flock   adored
The scars   the devastating voice

The scars were loved   and sparked in dreams
Great quantities of light   soon parted with

As arts no longer practiced   lost to name
Though even now today   would be recognized

Higher road   a clearing sky   an early mark that can't be
Wounded more   or burned or otherwise   destroyed

Ranging yesterday on horseback   low to land
Toward the barn the past   unchained

She was not beautiful but in a room
Filled with beautiful women   she killed their looks entirely

Even with its rancid aspects hers remained
Life   rather than death in life

Rapacious   changeful   free
Sleeping with doors open in case something might blow in

The grief that love can start all over again

St. Catherine of Siena

Knowing they couldn't get her whole body out of Rome,
The people of Siena stole off with her head.

What if most days ended up this way,
Both victorious and safe,

A father reading to his sons,
A mother moving from room to room
Putting folded clothes away,

The art dealer telexing the auction house
To demand a reliable provenance—

Where do whole lives come from, the voluminous
You and I?

As an anchoress she prayed be granted pain, three wounds.

Let us understand
She *asked for* suffering.

She is ours who are ridiculed for piety,
Ours in the house filled with lilies
When all the guests have gone

Hearing   *Daughter, this is what I want.*

          When the guards stopped them
And opened the bag   it was filled with roses.

YEAR OF THE HARROW

To afflict, as with an army.

Spring teeth
to pulverize and smooth.

After winter moths—

After winter months
breaking down the sauces
in the kitchen

Boarding the train
doubled over in a blast of grief.

At least this farm
I have visited

At least this far—

A blast like any other except
for what it opened

Hours in the dandelion
music, meal of tender vegetables
and jokes.

I went in love alone
to those infant joys.

Notes on the State of Virginia is the title of Thomas Jefferson's only book.

"In me as the swans" is a phrase from Plato's *Phaedo.*

Tomorrow I May Be Far Away is the title of Romare Bearden's 1967 Collage.

"No, Then Yes" — In *A Life of Poetry,* Muriel Rukeyser describes the pattern of her life as "no, then yes."

"Daresay"— Manteo is a town on Roanoke Island in North Carolina, the site of the first English attempt at colonizing America. The settlement became known as "The Lost Colony" after its more than 100 men, women and children disappeared, leaving no clues behind.

"Light a Candle, Put it Under a Bowl" is addressed to St. Catherine of Siena and owes a debt to Helen Vendler's essay on Hopkins in *The Breaking of Style,* in which she writes: "[Hopkins] dares to say even that the beautiful can teach us an important truth about the ethical, which is that the good must be at least as beautiful as the beautiful." The title is from the Book of Matthew 5:15.

"A Classical Answer" — The phrase "hysterically groomed" is Richard Howard's.

"Your city falls down so beautifully" is a remark made about the city of Baltimore by a cast member on the television show *The Wire.*

"Ecstatic Etymologies"— The four lines beginning with "She was not beautiful but in a room" are closely paraphrased from the excised text of *The Sun Also Rises* and from Harold Bloom's commentary on Brett Ashley.

ACKNOWLEDGMENTS

I am grateful to the editors of the journals in which some of these poems first appeared:

American Literary Review: "Dissection"
Center: "Open As"
The Cincinnati Review: "Acre"
Flyway: "Letter from Monticello, 1801"
Green Mountains Review: "So Long"
Gulf Coast: "Like Zelda"
Hawai'i Pacific Review: "The Brambles, the Glossy Black Fruit" (as "Blackberries")
Indiana Review: "In Which She Is Unmoving"
Journal of Medical Humanities: "On Her Knees in the Lettuce Bed"
Nebraska Review: "Night Swimming"
Phoebe: "Notes on the State of Virginia"
Poetry: "Fox in the Landscape," "In Me as the Swans"
The Saint Ann's Review: "Daresay"
Salamander: "Two Hydrogens, One Oxygen"
Salmagundi: "*Amaryllis* is an Alias"
Salt Hill: "To the Chinese the Peach Means Long Life"
Shenandoah: "The Rake," "Repeating Field," "September, Already"
Slate: "Be Honest"
Southern Poetry Review: "Parable," "Year of the Harrow"
The Southern Review: "On Finding One's Neighbor Dead in His Garden"
Third Coast: "Ephesus"
Tuesday; An Art Project: "Pond, the Vulnerable"

"The Famous Director Said *I love to see people coming out of darkness*" first appeared on the Massachusetts Cultural Council website.

"From the Top" first appeared (as "Above the Tree Line") in the Poetry Center of Chicago's Eighth Annual Juried Reading Chapbook and on the website.

Thank you to the Illinois Arts Council, the Massachusetts Cultural Council, the Poetry Society of America, the Ragdale Foundation, RopeWalk Writers' Retreat and the Schlesinger Writer-in-Residence Fund at St. Paul's School for generous support.

And with thanks for essential comments to Danielle Allen, Lucie Brock-Broido and all of the summer crew, Chris Car, Amy M. Clark, Jennifer S. Flescher, Sarah Gemmill, Jessica Green, William Harmon, Stephanie Kartalopoulos, Carol E. Miller, Kathy Nilsson, Martha Nussbaum, Gregory Orr, Mike Perrow, Jacquelyn Pope, Lynne Potts, Pamela Bailey Powers, Aimée Sands, Frank Solomon and Jonathan Weinert. And to my amazing family. And as ever, to Jack Goldsmith.

Photograph by Ira Jacobs

Leslie Williams is a recipient of the Poetry Society of America's Robert H. Winner Award and grants from the Illinois Arts Council and the Massachusetts Cultural Council. Her poems have appeared in *Poetry, Slate, The Southern Review, Shenandoah* and in many other magazines. A North Carolina native, she now lives near Boston with her husband and two sons.